I AM THE DAUGHTER TO THE KING

Royalty in Plain Sight

Tina Adams

"For You formed my innermost parts; You knit me [together] in my mother's womb. I will give thanks and praise to You for I am fearfully and wonderfully made; Wonderful are Your works, And my soul knows it very well." Psalm 139:13-14 Amp

This book, a culmination of a lifetime of tears, laughter, joy and sorrow, of prayer and discovery, is dedicated to each woman who has ever struggled with their identity or doubted their self-worth. I've certainly not reached the end of my journey, or learned everything there is to learn, and God continues to refine me each day. But what I have learned thus far, I would like to share with you. May the words on the pages to follow, and more importantly, His name, bring you comfort, healing, compassion, knowledge and wisdom as you discover your true identity as the Daughter to the King, Royalty in Plain Sight.

CONTENTS

INTRODUCTION

I recall sitting in my car on the corner of 8th and I Street in Washington D.C. with my children and two dogs while my husband enjoyed the comfort of a warm bed in our southern Maryland apartment. I pleaded on the telephone with the police to issue the emergency restraining order that had been granted earlier that day and remove my husband from the home as I had nowhere to go for the night. I was at the lowest point in my life.

It was like a scene from a movie. I met the police in a parking lot near our apartment. I told the kids to stay in the car until I came back. I was terrified!

The police instructed me to unlock the door to my apartment before they could legally enter and issue the restraining order. It was approximately 12:30 a.m. The police drew their guns and entered the pitch-dark apartment with their flashlights. I could hear them yelling my ex-husbands name and there was no response. I thought for a moment he may be dead; that he may have drank himself to death or overdosed on pills.

"How did I get here?" I thought to myself. I was in a deep dark pit that night. The police were able to wake my husband and successfully remove him from the apartment. As I stood in the parking lot of my apartment talking with the police, I received a death threat from my husband in a text on my cell phone; an obvious violation of the restraining order he had just been issued. The police escorted me to the courthouse where I spent the remainder of the night and early morning hours of the next day, filing out yet another complaint.

My journey began that night; the journey to healing, freedom, peace and finding out who I am in Him, in Christ.

I'm not sure what made you pick up this book, but I'm glad you did. I want you to know who you are in Christ and the power that is in His mighty name. Although my story starts in a pit, where you may be right now; there is freedom, healing, love, joy, and peace in knowing who you are in Him. Jesus is re-writing my story, and He can re-write yours as well.

My new journey started with surrender. Surrender to His will and His way. Each time I drift, I ask Him to remind me; I ask for knowledge, wisdom, and revelation. I continue to submit to

Him and ask for His guidance daily.

Getting out of the pit wasn't easy; and just like with any relationship, my relationship with Christ has taken work on my part. Papa continues to correct me today. Even in the process of writing this book, He has shown me that I need to deal with the shame I'm still holding onto. But Papa is a good, good Father and has always been patient and gentle with me.

In each of the chapters that follow, I will tell you more of my story. I'll tell you about the pit, but I will also tell you how I found my identity in Christ and His name; how He has been there for me, how He comforts me, how He has healed, restored and redeemed me. I'll take you on a journey out of the pit.

I invite you now to come along with me. My desire is to share my story with you and share the "good news;" all in His name and for His glory. My prayer is that you will also find who you are in Christ and His name. I pray you allow Papa to meet every need you have and fulfill your heart's desires.

CHAPTER 1

JEHOVAH NACHAM, THE LORD IS MY COMFORTER

It was supposed to be a fun weekend visit with my grandparents. The first evening went well, I suppose. The next morning, I awoke in the tight grip of his heavy arms nearly swallowing my little seven-year-old body. It was hot under the cover and his arms were moist with perspiration. My heart raced, and I felt like I couldn't breathe. Tom, my step-grandfather, wouldn't let go of me. I trembled with fear and cried with embarrassment as I began to urinate on him. My grandmother wasn't in the bed, or even the room. I began to panic. I tried to slip out from his arms, but he only tightened his grip and pulled me closer. He began to touch me in places no little girl should be touched. As Tom continued to fondle me, my thoughts raced. "How do I escape?" "What should I do?" "How do I make him stop?"

"I have to go to the bathroom," I exclaimed! He released

me from his clutch, and I made a dash for the bathroom. The bathroom was only feet from the bed. I quickly shut the door and locked it. I sat, crouched on the cold floor between the toilet and the bathtub; holding my knees to my chest, shivering and rocking back and forth. The walls were covered in a popular wallpaper for the 1970's with a raised velvety, pastel blue, floral print. I remember the scent of Dove soap, the pink bar of soap that smells like roses. I took deep breaths, inhaling the pleasing scent of that pink Dove soap and staring at those pastel blue walls. I began to soften my grip; and slowly I stopped shivering and rocking. I was still.

Looking back, I can see how God was there in that moment. I was still, in His presence. Jehovah Nacham, The Lord, my Comforter, was with me. He showed up in the decor and soothing pastel blue colors of the bathroom walls, and the scent of the Dove soap. It's amazing to me how God embraced me and soothed me while my little seven-year-old mind searched for understanding. God showed up in the physical, and in ways that would provide comfort in that very moment; comfort that would help me to breath, bring me peace and quite the storm. Jesus spoke to the winds and the waves, and I was still.

I don't know how long I was in the bathroom. It felt like quite a long time. I thought of how I could escape the room, how could I make it past the bed and to the bedroom door. Questions flooded my mind. "Should I yell?" "Will my grandmother hear me?" "Do I really want her to hear me?" "Do I really want to tell?" "Will she believe me?" "Will she be upset or angry?" "Will she be angry with me?"

Finally, I got the courage to open the bathroom door. I decided I would run for the bedroom door; it was only a few feet away. Tom looked like he was asleep, and I thought to myself, "I can make it." Tom wasn't sleeping. His arm reached out, barricading me in and blocking my path. He snatched me up, returning me to bed with him. I don't remember what happened next. My memory is blank. It is dark; black. There is nothing.

Loss of memory is common with a traumatic event. In fact, research indicates there are many after-effects of child sexual abuse. For example, interpersonal effects and relationship problems, problems with self-esteem and perception, depression, guilt, eating disorders and sexual problems. However, depression seems to be the most common long-term symptom among survivors.

God remains my comforter. He comforted me in the bathroom; soothed me and gave me His peace. Although I didn't understand it at the time, God helped me to rest in that moment in the bathroom. God, my Jehovah Nacham, comforts me today by erasing those memories from what was, and is possibly too much for me and that little seven-year-old girl to tolerate.

I have more memories of other occasions when Tom sexually abused me. However, most of the early years of my childhood are simply black; there's mostly nothing. I cannot tell you the names of my first grade, or second grade, or third grade, or even fourth grade teachers. I can't tell you if my teachers were male or female. I can't tell you about my school or my friends. I can't remember my birthdays. I have a few memories from my early childhood, but mostly, there's nothing. This memory loss is often referred to as a repressed memory; which is sometimes compared to dissociative amnesia. Dissociative amnesia is defined by the DSM-V as an "inability to recall autobiographical information."

I remain confident, Jehovah Nacham comforted me then, and continues to comfort me today. *"For this is what the Lord says: "I will extend peace to her like a river and the wealth of the nations like a flooding stream; you will nurse and be carried on her arm and dandled on her knees. As a mother comforts her child, so will I comfort you; and you will be comforted over Jerusalem." Isaiah 66:12-13*

I am a daughter to the King, and I find my comfort in Him. This revelation didn't happen in an instant for me, nor in a month, or even in a year's time. Your story will be different than mine, but, I encourage you to invite Him into your secret place; God desires to comfort you too.

"Those the Lord has rescued will return. They will enter Zion with singing; everlasting joy will crown their heads. Gladness and joy will overtake them, and sorrow and sighing will flee away. I, even I, am he who comforts you." Isaiah 51:11-12 Satan would have us focus on the pain of our wounds; fix our gaze on our past. The Word is truth, and the Word says, "Those the Lord has rescued will return." It may be difficult to comprehend, but this is already done, finished. The Lord *has* rescued you! You only need to be willing to receive the love, mercy and grace He has for you.

CHAPTER 2

JEHOVAH SHAMMAH,
THE LORD IS THERE

My parents had no idea that I was keeping this deep dark secret. They had no inkling that I harbored fear, hatred, and a deep sadness in my heart. I dared not tell a soul. I feared hurting my family. I feared being the source of anger, torment, destruction; and tearing the family apart. But most of all, I feared no one would believe me.

By the time I reached age ten the molestation stopped. This is also about the time where my childhood memories come into focus. At around age thirteen my grandmother and Tom moved in next door. I felt dirty and violated by his stare. He often tried to hug and hold me. Tom would slip his hand down the small of my back and grab me inappropriately. I remember thinking to myself, "doesn't anyone see this? Doesn't anyone see how he looks at me, how he touches me?!" I avoided Tom as much as possible. I avoided family gatherings and outings when he was present. It was during this time, at ages thirteen and fourteen that the memories of the sexual abuse began to become clear. This was the beginning of what would result in a deep depression for me, lasting many years to follow.

I became sexually active at the age of fourteen. I was promiscuous and sought attention from boys, and even men. I enjoyed the attention; I craved the attention, and affection. It was at that time in my life my dad began struggling with a demon of his own, alcoholism, a disease brought on by a combination of heredity and circumstance. My dad wasn't really present in my life during my teenage years. Dad would drink and do one of two things: get angry and argue, or pass-out. Mom did a lot of screaming; at Dad, at me, at my brothers. We all just existed trying to survive one day at a time, the best we knew how.

Some would ask, "Where are you God?" And there were probably times that I did ask. In the midst of a storm it is difficult to see clearly. But that is exactly where God is; our Jehovah Shammah is there, right in the middle of our storm. If you look, you can see him and feel him; in the whisper of a cool and crisp breeze; in the brilliant and beautiful colors of a sunrise, or the majestic gallop of wild stallions. I could go on describing all of God's beauty and majesty that surrounds us in the physical landscape He has provided, but God is also in us. *"To them God has chosen to make known among the Gentiles the glorious riches of this mystery, which is Christ in you, the hope of glory." Colossians 1:27* The "hope of glory" is in you. Do me a favor and pause for just a few minutes to let that sink in.

I do have some very fond memories of my childhood, like making recordings of singing "Louisiana Saturday Night" with my dad and brothers. And my first record player. The Barbie doll house my dad made for me. My mom making all my favorite dishes for a month just to get me to eat after having choked on a piece of steak; and rocking in my mother's lap as she tried to sooth me when I suffered from a severe ear infection. You see, God showed up in the physical, in my little world, through my parents and my brothers; the Lord my God was there.

Throughout my life, I can now see how God was there for me. He was there with me in that bathroom and He appears in the majestic beauty of nature that has always given me a calming peace. Through my mother's love, He was there for me when she realized the depth of my wounds and flew thousands of miles to be with me and comfort me at a time when I most needed her.

The Holy Spirit is in us, and we have authority in His name.

"For we are co-workers in God's service; you are God's field, God's building. By the grace God has given me, I laid a foundation as a wise builder, and someone else is building on it. But each one should build with care. For no one can lay any foundation other than the one already laid, which is Jesus Christ. If anyone builds on this foundation using gold, silver, costly stones, wood, hay or straw, their work will be shown for what it is, because the Day will bring it to light. It will be revealed with fire, and the fire will test the quality of each person's work. If what has been built survives, the builder will receive a reward. If it is burned up the builder will suffer loss but yet will be saved – even though only as one escaping through the flames. Don't you Know that you yourselves are God's temple and that God's Spirit dwells in your midst?" 1 Corinthians 3:11-16

As I said before, God shows up both in the spiritual and the physical; the supernatural and natural. However, we often take our focus off God and fix our gaze on the world around us in the middle of our storm. We allow Satan to distract us. We see what is going on in the natural and become distracted from God's promises. We can also fall into temptation and become distracted by things of the flesh; material wealth, objects, hobbies, etc. Unfortunately, we can become distracted and become trapped by sex, drugs and alcohol trying to self-medicate and control our circumstances, as I did as a young adult, by seeking the attention of men.

Our problems, circumstances, stress, etc. cause us to focus on the here and now; and we forget God is there with us, during our storm. God promises the return of His presence in Ezekiel 48:35 "... The Lord is there." God is our Jehovah Shammah.

I began dating a man when I was fourteen. He was eighteen and the older brother of a friend. He was out on his own, living in an apartment of his own. Looking back, I can see how I traded one tough situation for another. I wanted to escape the chaos of an alcoholic home and was desperate for what I thought was "love" from a man.

This relationship, if you can call it that, continued for many years. Two years into this relationship, at the age of sixteen, I became pregnant with my first child. I had been having unprotected sex for two years. I know I wanted out of my home; I pleaded with my mom to leave my dad many times. I think subconsciously I thought getting pregnant was my way out. However, when faced with the reality of having a baby, I became terrified of what was to come. How would it all work out? How would I take care of this baby? I was a junior in high school. I didn't have the means of taking care of myself, much less a baby.

I married at age sixteen, and two years later had my second child. I felt trapped. I was not equiped for caring for myself and my children. I believed my husband's threats to harm me and to take my children. I was very much controlled. I recall once being told I was not allowed to answer the telephone because it didn't belong to me since I didn't pay for anything.

I was kept dependent on my husband. He didn't want me to work outside of the home or go to school. We ended up moving two states away from my family and friends when I was twenty. Things were very much in the dark and hidden from everyone. I felt so alone at that time.

When my oldest daughter was five (and I was twenty-one), she began to display some concerning behavior, such as bed-wetting. She even stood in the doorway of her bedroom and urinated. Once she climbed onto the kitchen counter and urinated. Needless to say, I began bringing her to see a therapist.

The therapist soon let me know my daughter had been sexually abused. My five-year-old daughter had named her dad as her abuser. In less than twenty-four hours, I was gone. The therapists assisted me in reporting the abuse to the proper authorities and in planning my escape. It was truly an escape too. My parents and one of my brothers secretively drove fourteen hours through the night to meet me and my girls at the therapist's office the day after I found out about the abuse. Meanwhile, I had to pretend nothing was wrong so as not to let on to my husband that I was planning to leave. I was terrified.

I left the therapist's office that afternoon with my two girls. I went home and cooked dinner, did the dishes, bathed the children and put them to bed. Like I said, I pretended everything was fine.

The next morning, I was so anxious to leave and meet my parents and brother at the therapist's office. I made my husband's lunch and rushed him out the door claiming he would be late for work. As soon as my husband left for work, I gathered the girls and rushed off to meet my parents and brother. When I arrived at the therapist's office and set my eyes on my parents, I simply collapsed and wept uncontrollably. I had made it! I was going to be safe; my girls were going to be safe.

I remember being angry with God during this time. I could handle whatever came my way, but "God, why my baby girl?" I questioned. After years of being in an abusive marriage and finding out my ex-husband sexually abused our daughter, the marriage ended. It was then that I moved back into my parents' home with my two girls.

I wasn't aware of God's promises and my focus was so far off God at that time in my life. I continued down a path of destruction for many years to follow. But God was there. He was there in my parents embrace that morning in the therapist's office.

With every step in my journey, God was there and prepared me for a time such as this. A time when I would meet a woman at church who heard my testimony and approached me as she also experienced childhood sexual abuse. I would be able to empathize with her and connect with her in a way not many people could. A time when I would meet a woman who was in an abusive relationship and I would be able to provide guidance and encouragement. And without a doubt, a time when I would recognize and care for my own daughter because I had been there – God, Jehovah Shammah, had been there too.

CHAPTER 3

JEHOVAH ABBA, THE
LORD OUR FATHER

"Yet you, Lord, are our Father. We are the clay, you are the potter; we are all the work of your hand." Isaiah 64:8

I love this scripture! God is our father; our Jehovah Ab. Ab is the Aramaic origin of the Greek word Abba. Jesus cried out "Abba, Father." Matthew 14:36 Abba means *"daddy."* It is a very intimate term representing the relationship our heavenly father wants to have with each of us. God wants to be our daddy. We are each sons and daughters and have been adopted by God. We share an ineritance, as joint heirs to the Kingdom with Jesus. *"The Spirit you received does not make you slaves, so that you live in fear again; rather, the Spirit you received brought about your adoption to sonship. And by him we cry "Abba, Father."* Romans 8:15 We can call Him daddy, or pappa. We can curl up in the warmth of His embrace and talk to Him, cry to Him, or simply tell Him how our day is going.

Just as our earthly parents seek to guide us, give us direction and raise us into adulthood, our heavenly father wants this, and so much more for us. God is our daddy, and we can bring all that hurts and frustrates us, to Him. We can also share all that brings us joy, passion and excitement. God delights in us, His children, and wants to bring us healing and make us whole so that we can fulfill the unique purpose and plan He has for each of us. Scripture tells us this in Psalm 147:3, *"He heals the broken hearted and binds up their wounds."* Further, in Psalm 147:11, *"the Lord delights in those who fear Him, who put their hope in His unfailing love."* In other words, the Lord delights in those who have reverence and respect. If we revere and respect our earthly parents, how much more should we revere and respect our Abba.

I remember many times when my parent cared for me and bandaged a wound or brought me to the doctor and gave me medicine for an illness. Many of our wounds go deeper than a cut or a scrape. Our Abba wants to heal all our wounds. Just as our mom or dad cared for us (or perhaps it was a grandparent who cared for you), Abba, our heavenly daddy, wants to care for us.

So how did Abba heal my wounds? Very much the same way our earthly parents try to help us, and without fail. God has always been by my side, never wavering, never failing, never changing; maybe I didn't see it at the time, but I can see it now looking back. God provided a way; he gave His unconditional love, His grace and mercy... ALWAYS! And even though I fell and even walked away many times, He didn't. God was always right where *I* left Him. God healed my wounds when I turned to Him, when I decided to give my life to Him and make Him the focus of everything in my life. Then, and only then, did I begin to find freedom and healing of all the wounds; whether self-inflicted by my own sin, or healing from the wounds created by the sin of others in my life.

While God can heal us in an instant, most often our healing takes place over time. For me, healing took place over decades. I believe that the Lord allowed me to remember and address my wounds when He knew I was ready. He would have a person cross my path, or I would have an encounter that would help me to peel back a layer and gently open the wound slightly. These encounters would be a song, a conversation, or a passage of scripture that would speak to me in a way like never before. This is how the Holy Spirit will speak to you too, as long as you invite Him in.

As we submit to the Father, and allow him to peel back the layers, we experience a deeper, inner healing. As we open our hearts, our minds, our eyes, and our ears to the subtle and gentle nudges of the Holy Spirit, we can take another step toward healing and freedom. *"Now the Lord is the Spirit, and where the Spirit of the Lord is, there is freedom."* 2 Cor 3:17   Often times, however, we don't want to take the time, or put forth the effort in our healing process. Sometimes we don't want to experience the pain felt in the healing process. We prefer to be microwaved on high for 4 to 6 minutes; sound familiar. Our Father on the other hand is a Potter.

Unlike the instant results of a microwave oven, molding pottery takes time. After the potter shapes the clay into its creation, the clay goes through a firing process that can take many hours. In the case of each of us, this process can take a lifetime. Romans 12:2 says *"Do not conform to the pattern of this world but be transformed by the renewing of your mind. Then you will be able to test and approve what God's will is – His good, pleasing and perfect will."* When we renew our minds through an intimate relationship with Abba, we continue to be transformed.

Are you willing to take the next step in your journey? No matter the pain you have experienced, no matter the questions you may have, all the answers to all our questions and the healing from our wounds can be found in His name; and of all the names of God, Jehovah Ab may be one of the most significant as it surmises who we are in Christ, and how we should relate to and be in relationship with God as our Father, our Abba, Papa, our Daddy.

CHAPTER 4

JEHOVAH SHA'AG TSIYOWN, THE LORD SHALL ROAR OUT OF ZION

After having found out my daughter had been sexually abusedby my husband, I moved back into my parent's home with my two girls just after my 22nd birthday. While this living arrangement helped me (and was really my only option at the time), it meant I had to live next door to Tom. It was then that I finally told my parents about the sexual abuse I had experienced as a child. I wasn't necessarily ready to tell my parents, but I was determined to protect my children from Tom. I needed to explain to my parents why my children would never be allowed to go next door.

Things didn't go exactly the way I had hoped. I believe my parents were shocked. My mother asked me to keep everything a secret as much as possible and not to tell my grandmother. My mother didn't want to upset my grandmother and I know now, she truly believed that this news would literally kill my grandmother. Fear is crippling, and I believe my mother was crippled with fear. A Spirit of Fear ruled over all of us back then.

I was 22, when I first told my parents of the sexual abuse, and I kept my secret from my grandmother until I was 32, because my mother requested that I do so.

I was angry, very angry; at my abuser, at my parents, at my brothers, at my grandmother, and of course Tom ... I was very angry for a very long time. It appeared everyone was pretending nothing ever happened. My family celebrated birthdays and holidays with this man, Tom. He was welcome in my parents' home, which crushed me. I felt so betrayed. My brothers and their families would attend these family gatherings and I was so confused by it all. I felt like an outsider and that no one was on my side (and I wanted someone on my side!)

My heart hardened. I refused to show mercy or grace toward anyone. I refused to forgive. I was determined that the only one I could count on was me. I was determined that I didn't need anyone.

"The Lord will roar from Zion and thunder from Jerusalem; the earth and the heavens will tremble. But the Lord will be a refuge for his people, a stronghold for the people of Israel." Joel 3:16 *"In that day the mountains will drip new wine, and the hills will flow with milk; all*

the ravines of Judah will run with water. A fountain will flow out of the LORD's house and will water the valley of acacias." Joel 3:18, And there came a day when the Lord roared for me, the earth trembled for me and the Lord shook me. I knew I could take refuge in His arms.

God promises that one day all evil in the world will be destroyed. God came for me, roaring, in full force! Like a mama bear protecting her cub, Abba came for me. He met me right where I was, in all my mess, ready to protect me, ready to pour out His amazing love, mercy and grace. God met me in the pit and carried me out. He loved on me, healed my wounds, and made me new.

It's ok to be angry, and it's even righteous. Even Jesus got angry. *"It was nearly time for the Jewish Passover celebration, so Jesus went to Jerusalem. In the Temple area he saw merchants selling cattle, sheep, and doves for sacrifices; he also saw dealers at tables exchanging foreign money. Jesus made a whip from some ropes and chased them all out of the Temple. He drove out the sheep and cattle, scattered the money changers' coins over the floor, and turned over their tables. Then going over to the people who sold doves, he told them, "Get these things out of here. Stop turning my Father's house into a marketplace!"* John 2:13-16

It isn't a sin to be angry, it is how we handle our anger that most often results in sin. *"And don't sin by letting anger control you.*

Don't let the sun go down while you are still angry, for anger gives a foothold to the devil." Ephesians 4:26-27 NLT

We are made in God's image, and therefore we can emulate the same desires and characteristics of God. It's ok to ROAR at the evil in the world, as long as we do not allow ourselves to be consumed by anger. I had allowed myself to be consumed by anger and it held me captive. While it was ok to have the feelings of hurt, confusion, betrayal and anger, I let it consume me. That darkness robbed me of years with my family that I of course blamed Tom for; but today I see more clearly. I see, and know my family was responding the only way they knew how, and I was too. I'm glad I know a better way now.

God wants us to be consumed by Him. His all-consuming fire. He wants to flush out and remove all the bad in a consuming fire, purifying us, and replace it with His love, mercy, forgiveness ... all that is life-giving. Will you submit to His will for you and your life? God will ROAR for you, if you allow Him.

CHAPTER 5

JEHOVAH OWZ ZIMRATH, THE LORD IS MY STRENGTH AND MY SONG

It was one thing to tell my parents of the sexual abuse I had experienced as a young child, but to begin to tell my story to others has been a very different experience all together. When I told my parents, it was out of necessity and to keep my children safe. But I wasn't prepared to deal with that demon, much less the one that would rear its ugly head when I faced rejection through a request to remain silent and continue to keep very dark secrets. For years Satan whispered in my ear of how all my fears came true. I prayed my children would be safe from such abuse, and yet, my daughter was also sexually abused. I feared if I ever told anyone my family would be torn, and it was. My family was divided. For years, over a decade, I didn't attend family celebrations where Tom was in attendance. It was lonely; I felt like an outcast and lived a life separate from my family. Satan whispered, "you see, I told you so; you should have kept your mouth shut!" "You are not what's important here, look what you are doing to your family!" I remained in a very dark place for many years before I could even begin to imagine that I was deserving of love.

God's word is full of His promises. His word says, *"The Spirit of the Lord God is upon me, because the Lord has anointed me to bring good news to the poor; he has sent me to bind up the brokenhearted, to proclaim liberty to the captives, and the opening of the prison to those who are bound; to proclaim the year of the Lord's favor, and the day of vengeance of our God; to comfort all who mourn; to grant to those who mourn in Zion - to give them a beautiful headdress instead of ashes, the oil of gladness instead of mourning, the garment of praise instead of a faint spirit; that they may be called oaks of righteousness, the planting of the Lord, that he may be glorified."* Isaiah 61:1-3 ESV

It was ten years after I first told my parents about the sexual abuse I suffered as a child, that I stood tall and allowed the strength of the Lord to help me confront my abuser. I was in my early thirties. As God walked with me and strengthen me, as He mended my broken heart, He did the same for those around me.

My mother came with me and stood by my side as I confronted Tom. I had written him a letter and simply requested he listen to me while I read the letter to him. Tom began to interrupt me and I'll never forget his words ... "Well I don't remember doing these things, but if I was drunk and I did these things, I'm sorry." My mother jumped in and told Tom to "Shut up!" She told him to stop talking and just listen! I was projected and covered by God's grace, mercy and love in my mother's presence and defense of me.

My mother was no longer riddled with fear ; rather she was courageous and bold. My dad had battled alcoholism and has remained sober for over 30 years now. God was proclaiming favor and the day of vengeance; He was comforting all who mourned!

As I grew in my understanding of who I am in Christ, who God says that I am, I sang His praises, and continue to sing His praises today. Song, worship, music that glorifies God, ushers us into His presence; and in His presence, there is mighty strength! What is so amazing to me, as I look back and recall the series of events that led to a shift for me, and

my family, it all started with worship; literally! I began singing in a praise and worship band just months before con-
fronting Tom.

As it is written in 2 Kings 3:14-15, in the Amplified
version, *"Elisha said, "As the Lord of hosts (armies) lives, before
whom I stand, were it not that I have regard for Jehoshaphat
king of Judah, I would not look at you nor see you [king of Israel].
But now bring me a musician." And it came about while the
musician played, that the hand (power) of the Lord came upon
Elisha."* It was after the musician played, that the power of
the Lord came! As I sang praise to the Lord, He strengthened
me, and the power of the Lord, His hand was upon me!

God captured my heart, told me who I am, gave me beauty
for ashes, and by doing so, strengthened me. I sing His praises;
and with every song, I enter His courts and become ever closer
to Him, my Abba. All things that were lost, are now found. As
the daughter the King of Kings, I have purpose; and it was only
through my relationship with Abba, that I have come to understand, and to tell my story with boldness.

When the trumpet blast broke the walls around the city
of Jericho, battle followed; and just like in Jericho, I fought many
more battles. At age 32 I was married to my second husband. Fast

forward 6 years and two more failed and abusive, dysfunctional marriages later (the last ending with a restraining order and the police removing my ex-husband from our home in the middle of the night), I found myself at the bottom of my pit. I was tired, depressed and becoming desperate; but not beaten! I am more than a conqueror, I am a victor. Our God is so faithful. He remained with me every step of the way, through each and every battle I faced. The Lord is my song and gives me strength!

CHAPTER 6

JAHOVAH RAPHA, THE
LORD YOUR HEALER

God has always been present in my life, but I haven't always seen clearly enough to recognize Him; this may be true for you as well. In the summer of 2011, I was 38 years old and had recently divorced my fourth husband. God's light was brighter than ever and all the sudden I could see – clearly (well more clearly – I'm a work in progress). God was not going to give up on me; He won't give up on any of us. God will finish the work He began in you. I needed healing. I fixed my gaze on Jehovah Rapha, the Lord my Healer!

1 Peter 2:9 says, *"But you are a chosen people, a royal priesthood, a holy nation, God's special possession, that you may declare the praises of Him who called you out of darkness into His wonderful*

light." God called me out of the darkness and into His wonderful light, and thus began a healing within me.

I confessed my sins ... literally; a lifetime of sins. I grew up Catholic, so I went where I knew to go and took the first step toward a relationship with Jesus; a true and intimate relationship. I reached out to a friend and she went with me to confession at the nearest Catholic Church. I felt Jesus' presence, His truly amazing grace and mercy. Jesus spoke to me that day; He was so kind, gentle and forgiving.

I started to invite Jesus into my life, into my heart; into those broken and shattered places of my heart. I turned to God to make me whole, to complete me – instead of another relationship, another man (as I had done so many times before). Jesus said in John chapter 11, as he spoke to Martha, the sister of Lazarus ... "whoever believes in me will live even if he dies." To believe means to trust. It was during this season in my life that I entrusted my life to Jesus. To entrust your life to Jesus will bring more that healing; it will bring an indiscribable peace.

I wanted to get to know God, my Father, my Abba. I pleaded with him to show me the way. I pleaded, "show me how to seek you Abba, where to seek you!" I began reading the Bible again and reading books on how to study scripture. I desperately wanted to know God and be in an intimate relationship with him. I never want to leave His embrace again! I love the feeling of resting in my Father's arms. Papa always knows what I need.

God promises in Exodus 16:26, *"If you will diligently listen to the voice of the Lord your God, and do that which is right in his eyes, and give ear to his commandments and keep all the statutes, I will put none of the diseases on you that I put on the Egyptians, for I am the Lord, your healer."* But God is not just the healer of physical ailments. Jehovah Rapha is the healer of our hearts. He wants to heal and restore us; He wants to exchange beauty for ashes.

If only we keep His commandments, if only we seek His guidance and will for our lives, if only we would turn and run home to Him.

"And he said, 'There was a man who had two sons. And the younger of them said to his father, "Father, give me the share of property that is coming to me. And he divided his property between them. Not many days later, the younger son gathered all he had and took a journey into a far country, and there he squandered his property in reckless living. And when he had spent everything, a severe famine arose in the country, and he began to be in need. So he went and hired himself out to one of the citizens of that country, who sent him into his fields to feed pigs. And he was longing to be fed with the pods that the pigs ate, and no one gave him anything.

But when he came to himself, he said, 'How many of my father's hired servants have more than enough bread, but I perish here with hunger! I will arise and go to my father, and I will say to him, "Father, I have sinned against heaven and before you. I am no longer worthy to be called your son. Treat me as one of your hired servants." And he arose and came to his father. But while he was still a long way off, his father saw him and felt compassion, and ran and embraced him and kissed him. And the son said to him, 'Father, I have sinned against heaven and before you. I am no longer worthy to be called your son. But the father said to his servants, bring quickly the best robe, and put it on him, and put a ring on his hand, and shoes on his feet. And bring the fattened calf and kill it and let us eat and celebrate. For this my son was dead, and is alive again; he was lost, and is found. And they began to celebrate. Luke 15:11-24, ESV

Oh, how our Father wants to heal us and restore us to the sons and daughters He created us to be. His love is infinite - endless! Let that sink in. Our God is infinite, and his love is so great He shows up for us, loves on us, listens to us, and sits with us. Think of the many brothers and sisters we have; our God's love never ends and therefore He has enough for each of us. Give Him a chance. Seek Him, and He will meet you where you are, summon for a robe a ring for your finger and prepare a celebration for you. The summer of 2011, I spent hours in the word and fell in love with Jesus, my God and my Papa. His word has the power to mend our wounds. It was during that three-month period God penetrated my heart of stone. He revealed to me that I am the daughter to the King, I am royalty. I am the crown of creation.

I felt like the prodigal son from the story told in Luke Chapter 15, the night I went to confession; the night I laid everything down and called out to Jesus to save and heal me. On the night I went to confession I began my journey to know the Lord in a much different way. I was learning to be in an intimate relationship with Him. When I hit a bump in the road, I'm reminded that God is not done with me yet. He continues to restore, polish and refine me daily. But oh, what freedom I find in His presence and how awesome it is to rest in Him, knowing and trusting that He is in control.

CHAPTER 7

JAHOVAH CHECED, THE LORD
IS MERCIFUL AND GRACIOUS

God has a plan for me and he continues to reveal his plan through songs, conversations, and scripture. He has even displayed His love for me on the side of a building. Literally on the side of a building on 16th Street NW, in Washington DC. There it was, Jeremiah 29:11, which says,

"FOR I KNOW THE PLANS I
HAVE FOR YOU," DECLARES

THE LORD, "PLANS TO PROSPER YOU AND NOT TO HARM YOU, PLANS TO GIVE YOU HOPE AND A FUTURE."

The Lord "declared" it - He declared I was His, and He had good plans for me. It was the spring of 2011 (I'm backing up just a bit to right before that awful night when my ex-husband was removed from our apartment in the middle of the night). God used the side of a building to get my attention. I was on my way home from work, had just stepped off the bus and was walking the rest of the way to my apartment. This was my routine. The same bus, the same walk home.

I landed myself in yet another abusive relationship and recall very clearly saying to myself, "This is just all there is for me; This is just the way life is; I need to just accept that this is all there is and accept being in an abusive relationship." I told myself, "Just suck it up Tina, quit complaining."

Moments later I passed the building with Jeremiah 29:11, plastered to the entire side of it. The words of this scripture filled the entire side of this building. It had to measure at least 40-foot-wide by 80 to 100 foot tall; at least this is how it appeared to me. God pulled out His bullhorn and shouted, "I have plans for you Tina! Good plans! My plan is not to harm you! I have plans to give you hope and a future!" God was willing to use a bullhorn with me, and He is coming after you as well.

Fast forward now, through many months of prayer, meditation, study and time with the Lord, I discovered the desires God placed in my heart. I struggled to embrace these desires as a blessing and actually asked God to take them from me at one time. My desires for as long as I could remember were to be a wife and mother (a mother of four to six children to be exact). But this desire and my attempts to have this in my life had failed, time and time again. This desire had brought me nothing but pain, or so I thought. I made the following journal entry in October 2011.

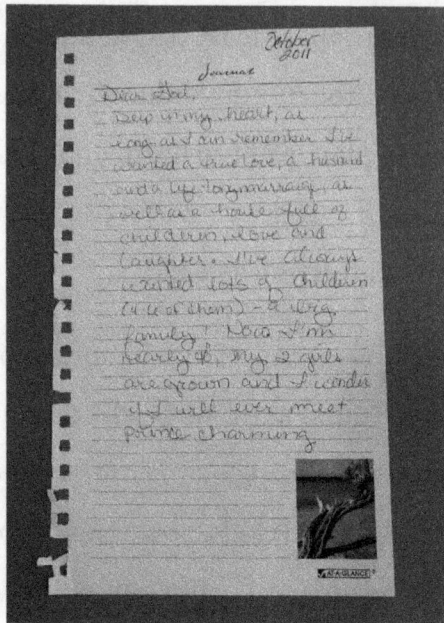

"Dear God, Deep in my heart, as long as I can remember I've wanted a tue love, a husband and a life-long marriage, as well as a house full of children, love and laughter. I've always wanted lots of children (4-6 of them) - a big family! Now I'm nearly 40, my 2 girls are grown, and I wonder if I will ever meet Prince Charming."

One afternoon while perusing the Christianity section at Barnes and Noble, and although I had read the book before, God led me to read it again; *Captivating*, by John and Staci Eldredge. This time, I was ready to receive; ready for the healing Jesus had for me. This book speaks to a woman's heart and who God created you, as woman, created in His image, to be.

I began to see myself as God sees me, captivating. But for a long time, my wounded heart distorted my view. Many women forget, or never realize that they are created in the image of God. I had forgotten.

Although I slipped up and continue to do so from time to time today, God is so merciful and gracious! In our darkness, in our sin, God continues to have mercy and forgiveness for us.

"They refused to obey and were not mindful of the wonders that you performed among them, but they stiffened their neck and appointed a leader to return to their slavery in Egypt. But you are a God ready to forgive, gracious and merciful, slow to anger and abounding in steadfast love, and did not forsake them." Nehemiah 9:17 ESV

We must also forgive. Unforgiveness keeps us in sin; in bondage. Unforgiveness hardens our hearts. Forgiveness for the man who abused me and robbed me of innocence at such a young age, was very hard for me. It didn't happen overnight. It has been a process; and just when I thought I had forgiven, God revealed yet another place in my heart where I continued to harbor ill feelings for this person; where I still clung to the pain and sadness. I truly grieved over the loss of my innocence, and the loss of relationship with family for many years. All those years I remained silent at the request of my parents, I also remained absent. I stayed far away; away from family gatherings, birthday celebrations and Christmas dinners. I had lost out on precious time being in relationship with my family. I had to grieve that loss.

It wasn't until I was able to forgive that I was set free of the chains sin keeps us all locked in. Satan would have us stay in darkness. Satan would have me keep secrets; keep my distance and remain out of relationship.

Things that are hidden are in darkness. God is light, and when we allow Him to come in and shine His light on our problems, our circumstances, our hurts ... we come into the light. We find freedom in the light.

When we forgive, we aren't saying what has been done is okay, we are just coming into the light and bringing our problems, our circumstances, and our hurts, to God so He can shine light on us. God's light is life-giving.

When are hearts are hardened, it's like we are frozen solid. If we allow God to shine on us and our hearts, the light softens our hearts; we defrost so to speak. Let the truth and the light of God defrost you and warm your heart! And bring life to the areas in your life that are dark, hardened and frozen.

Receive the mercy and grace He has for you and extend that same mercy and grace to others. *"Get rid of all bitterness, rage and anger, brawling and slander, along with every form of malice. Be kind and compassionate to one another, forgiving each other, just as in Christ God forgave you."* Ephesians 4:31-32

My prayer is that these are words of encouragement and hope; not a standard by which you are expected to live 100 percent of the time. Even though I have grown and matured in my walk with Christ, there are days I get offended, and fall short; I miss the mark sometimes. Do not be discouraged when you miss the mark. Resist the negative self-talk Satan would have you listen to, and that sends you into a downward spiral, and away from Christ. The best way to remain on track is to remain in His Word and in Him. Renew your mind daily (throughout the day if necessary – and sometimes it *is* absolutely necessary!).

The armor of God is the only way to be prepared to battle all this world, and our enemy would have you focus on. It is paramount that you continue to drink of His Word to battle the temptations of the flesh and falling back to old ways where offense sets in and unforgiveness hardens your heart, where mercy and grace are nowhere to be found.

The Armor of God

[10] In conclusion, be strong in the Lord [draw your strength from Him and be empowered through your union with Him] and in the power of His [boundless] might. [11] Put on the full armor of God [for His precepts are like the splendid armor of a heavily-armed soldier], so that you may be able to [successfully] stand up against all the schemes and the strategies and the deceits of the devil. [12] For our struggle is not against flesh and blood [contending only with physical opponents], but against the rulers, against the powers, against the world forces of this [present] darkness, against the spiritual forces of wickedness in the heavenly (supernatural) places. Ephesians 6:10-12 AMP

Just as soldiers prepare for battle in the natural, we must be prepared and protected in the supernatural and heavenly realm. Although it is unseen by our natural eyes (the flesh), there is a real battle going on and we must have protection to engage in that battle. A soldier would not go out to the battlefield without his protective gear that helps to shield him from the enemy's advances and attack. We should not think any differently about our spiritual protection when engaging in spiritual warfare.

[13] Therefore, put on the complete armor of God, so that you will be able to [successfully] resist and stand your ground in the evil day [of danger], and having done everything [that the crisis demands], to stand firm [in your place, fully prepared, immovable, victori-

ous]. [14] So stand firm and hold your ground, having tightened the wide band of truth (personal integrity, moral courage) around your waist and having put on the breastplate of righteousness (an upright heart), [15] and having strapped on your feet the gospel of peace in preparation [to face the enemy with firm-footed stability and the readiness produced by the good news]. [16] Above all, lift up the [protective] shield of faith with which you can extinguish all the flaming arrows of the evil one. [17] And take the helmet of salvation, and the sword of the Spirit, which is the Word of God. Ephesians 6:13-16 AMP

Without the "band of truth" we will not be able to discern the lies of our enemy. Jesus is the way, the truth and the life. The only way to the Father is through Jesus. Knowing God, and the truth, helps us to identify what is not the truth. The heart is a vital organ and where the springs of life flow. The "breastplate of righteousness" guards your heart. We are made right with God through Jesus Christ. Jesus died for us and issues you a breastplate of righteousness to protect you from evil when you give your life to Him. Strapping on your feet the "gospel of peace" speaks to standing firm and being rooted; unshakeable by the enemy.

18 With all prayer and petition pray [with specific requests] at all times [on every occasion and in every season] in the Spirit, and with this in view, stay alert with all perseverance and petition [interceding

in prayer] for all God's people. Ephesians 6:18 AMP

I implore you to read this scripture aloud daily and imagine readying yourself for battle. These are gifts that God gave each of us for our protection. Why wouldn't you want to have His protection?

Putting on the "Armor of God" readies us for the battle against temptations of the flesh, protects us from offense and will enable us to forgive. Often, we don't think of forgiveness in terms of forgiving ourselves. We must also forgive ourselves. One might find this concept odd, but in many instances, we find it more difficult to forgive ourselves than others. We can speak such harsh words over ourselves and our own situations that we would never consider speaking over others. Many of us need to take time to allow God's mercy and grace to fall on us and that can be harder to do than pouring out His mercy and grace on others. Why? Well for me personally, forgiving myself required me to be vulnerable and take a look at my wounds. This is something I didn't want to do for a long time, nor have I ever met anyone who was jumping at the chance to open an old festering wound.

In order to forgive myself, I had to be willing to be vulnerable with God. I had to trust that my Abba truly loved me and all my mess. It's a hard concept to grasp, Grace. "In Him we have redemption that is, our deliverance and salvation, through His blood, which paid the penalty for our sin and resulted in the forgiveness and complete pardon of our sin, in accordance with the riches of His grace which He lavished on us." Ephesians 1:7 AMP He has lavished grace on us. The word lavish means generous and extravagant. God generously pours out His grace on us in an extravagant way!

So how did I forgive myself; how did I allow myself to become vulnerable with God? Just like in any relationship, I took time to get to know God. I spend time in the word and in prayer. I talk to God and we have built a relationship that becomes stronger everyday. In doing this I continue to let go of the past, forgive myself, and look forward to what God has in store for me. Paul tells us this in Philippians. "Brothers and sisters, I do not consider myself yet to have taken hold of it. But one thing I do: Forgetting what is behind and straining toward what is ahead, I press on toward the goal to win the prize for which God has called me heavenward in Christ Jesus." Phil 3:13-14

I look forward to becoming all that God created me to be. I am the daughter to the King, made new in Him. "Therefore, if anyone is in Christ, he is a new creation. The old has passed away; behold, the new has come." 2 Cor 5:17 ESV

CHAPTER 8

JEHOVAH HALAL, THE LORD IS WORTHY TO BE PRAISED

I sit in amazement at how God has written these pages. I speak of understanding, and having the strength to boldly tell my story; why? Because He is worthy to be praised! I give all the glory, all the praise and honor to my God, my Abba, the King of Kings!

My hope is that as you read the words on these pages, you will come to know God through my story, that you will see Him how I see Him, and grow in relationship with Him. My hope is that you will experience the freedom and peace only found in the presence of the Living God.

God is worthy, and he keeps His promises. Those desires He

sets in your heart before you were formed in your mother's womb, He will fullfill; if you work with Him. Belief, trust, faith .... require action.

I want to shout from a mountain top all that God has done for me; and more importantly than my desire to praise Him, is my desire to *obey* God and share my story with others who will be changed by the words on these pages. If only one person comes to know God, and not just know about God, but grow in an intimate relationship with Him, I know He will be well pleased.

Matthew 28:19-20 (AMP) says, *"Go therefore and make disciples of all the nations [help the people to learn of Me, believe in Me, and obey My words], baptizing them in the name of the Father and of the Son and the Holy Spirit, teaching them to observe everything that I have commanded you; and lo, I am with you always [remaining with you perpetually – regardless of circumstance, and on every occasion], even to the end of the age."*

This is not a "self-help" book. There is nothing we can do, accomplish, succeed at, or complete, on our own. Matthew 19:26 says, "Jesus looked at them and said, 'With man this is impossible, but with God all things are possible.'" This is why I give praise to God. It is only through Him that I am able, that I am strengthened, that I find comfort and peace.

As I said before, when the walls of Jericho fell , Joshua and the Israelites faced many more battles. After I confronted my abuser, Tom, I fought more battles. The battle of depression, the battle of guilt and the battle of shame. But God remained with me perpetually, regardless of my circumstances and on every occasion; always. He is worther to be praised!

We do not have to do all the work; actually God never intended for us to do all the work. Sometimes our circumstances look grim and feel heavy. God wants to cary the burden for us. That isn't to say that we won't face troubles or that we won't ever have to do any work. What I'm saying is that we need to lift only what God intended for us to lift and do only the work he has already quipped us to do. He prepares us, equips us and trains us to do the work He asks of us, and He does the rest. Things go wrong (terribly wrong) when we step out of our lane and try to accomplish everything in our own will and strength. Praise God it doesn't have to be this way!

The enemy uses fear to get us off track. We get off track, we become fearful, and we don't trust God to stand in the gap for us. When we don't trust God and are determined to do things in our own strength, we are essentially thinking of ourselves as God. Think about it; we step out of our lane and into God's lane, trying to accomplish what only He can accomplish in, through and for us.

There are many scripture references for resting. Jesus tell us in Matthew 11:28, "Come to me, all you who are weary and burdened, and I will give you rest." Praise God we have such a good Father who wants to cary our burdens while we rest.

CHAPTER 9

JEHOVAH OWR YESHA, THE LORD IS MY LIGHT AND MY SALVATION

I've lived most of my life in fear. Fear of the chaos I faced daily, growing up in an alcoholic home; fear of rejection, fear of abuse, fear of telling the truth ... the list goes on, and on. Satan had a field day with me and my fears; fanning the flame of fear for so many years and diminishing my hope. But that was before I knew Jesus, before I met my Abba.

Psalm 27:1-9 (AMP) says *"The Lord is my light and my salvation – Whom shall I fear? The Lord is the refuge and fortress of my life – Whom shall I dread? When the wicked came against me to eat up my flesh, my adversaries and my enemies, they stumbled and fell. Though an army encamp against me, my heart will not fear; though war arise against me, even in this I am confident."*

Satan wants us to remain in the dark; keep our wounds a secret, to run, and to hide. The Lord is our "light" in the darkness! Jesus yearns to be in relationship with us; like one yearns for her beloved. When we allow Him, when we invite Him, when we submit to Him – all is brought out of the darkness and into the light. When we are in His presence, we are in the light. When we are in the light, we receive salvation! When we receive, we invite the light in and we become the light in a world of darkness. We are Christ's hands and feet and His light shines in and through us. We have nothing to ever fear for our God is a good, good Father! Even though our circumstances may seem bleak, our enemy will fall in the presence of the Almighty and His light!

In Psalm 27, the scripture says, *"my enemies, they stumbled and fell."* Stumbled means to trip and fell means to leave an erect position suddenly and involuntarily. Another definition of "fell" is to drop down wounded or dead; to die in battle. This means that in the presence of the Lord our enemy literally "drops dead!" How awesome is that? Does that not give you comfort, confidence and courage?

No matter your situation, the Lord can shine His light on you, and the enemy will drop dead; the enemy has no authority over you.

Salvation means to be delivered from harm, ruin, or loss.

You and I have been bought, and Jesus paid a hefty price. I have nothing to fear, and neither do you. Our Lord is our light and our salvation. Jesus paid the price. John 19:30 says, *"When He received the drink, Jesus said, 'It is finished.' With that He bowed His head and gave up His Spirit."* The word *finished* is the same as paid in full. Jesus paid the price for our salvation and paid in full.

All of my life I've known who Jesus was, but there is a difference between knowing of someone, and "knowing" someone. I probably really started to know Jesus and be in relationship with Him all those years ago when I joined the praise and worship team. I am so thankful that God is faithful, and He continued to shine a light on my path. He was with me through every battle, every failure, and forgave every sin even as He patiently waited for me to willingly submit my life, all of me, to Him. Until the summer of 2011. Does this mean I will never fall again? Of course not. I trip up and sin daily, and Papa is ready and waiting to forgive me every time I repent of my sin. The Potter is not done with me yet. He continues to shape and mold me. I walk with my head held high knowing He loves me, He is the light to my path and my salvation.

CHAPTER 10

JEHOVAH IMMANUEL, THE
LORD GOD IS WITH US

Our enemy would have us believe we are alone. Just as I am sure you have felt alone, so did I ... many, many times. Our enemy is the "father of lies." The enemy whispers words of shame and guilt in our ears. We listen and begin to believe that we aren't worthy, that the things we have done (or the things that have been done to us) are worse than anything anyone has ever done ... and we stay in the dark. We are never alone, never. Jehovah Immanuel, the Lord God is with us always.

Isaiah 7:14 (AMP) says *"Therefore, the Lord Himself will give you a sign: Listen carefully, the virgin will conceive and give birth to a son, and she will call his name Immanuel (God is with us)."* God came to live with and among us; and now lives in us. The living God, our

Abba, lives in, and is with each of us.

During what I believe was one of the lowest, most desperate moments in my life, God revealed himself to me through a stranger, a large African American woman. If you have every read *The Shack*, by WM. Paul Young, you know the author depicts God as a large African American woman. God, our heavenly Father, the almighty creator of heaven and earth came to me, to put His arms around me and be with me.

It was a Friday night in May 2011, and I was out to dinner with my best friend and my daughters. The week had been long and grueling. I had appeared in court for a final hearing on a restraining order against my ex-husband. I had been terrified and hiding out in a model apartment until the apartment complex could change the locks on the doors to my apartment. I could barely keep myself together. I smoked back then and excused myself from the table to go outside for a cigarette.

I was in a world of my own, a daze, I felt like (and probably looked like) a zombie. I sat on a bench outside the restaurant, lit a cigarette with my hands shaking uncontrollably and took a deep drag. Tears streaming, I sat and finished my cigarette. All the while I hadn't noticed a woman sitting on the bench adjacent to me. She tried to engage me in conversation and I'm not certain what she asked, but as I stood to walk away and return to dinner, she stood and stopped me. What she said next, I heard loud and clear. The woman told me God told her to give me a hug and that nothing is too big for God. It was at that moment I really got a good look at this woman and I let her hug me. I stood in her embrace weeping for what seemed like an eternity, but it was only for a moment. I thanked her and returned to my dinner.

When I got to my table I immediately told my friend what happened and asked her to come outside with me. To my surprise the woman was gone and nowhere to be found. Now it's not like this woman could easily disappear into a crowd. She was a large woman, dressed in brilliantly gold and turquoise colored, authentic African apparel. FYI, the color gold symbolizes glory, divinity and kingship; and the color turquoise signifies the healing power of God. I am convinced God himself was with me that night and allowed me to rest in His embrace as He shielded me and comforted me from the terrifying world around me. God reminded me that I most certainly was *not* alone.

CHAPTER 11

JEHOVAH MIBTACH, THE
LORD IS MY TRUST

Psalm 71:5-6, says "For you have been my hope, Sovereign Lord, my confidence since my youth. From birth I have relied on you; you brought me forth from my mother's womb. I will ever praise you." What God did for David is promised to us. We can rely on God and trust in Him.

Our God is so good, and faithful! How do we move forward? What comes after forgiveness? When we have been wounded, it is often hard to love and trust again. We can do this because we can trust in the Lord; because He loves us, because He is our joy, our peace, and He will sustain us. We don't have to be afraid. We can trust in the Lord.

It wasn't until I finally gave my life to Jesus, submitted to His will for me and sought Him first, that my heart's desire was met. I sought God to complete me and make me whole. I realized that no man can do for me what God can do. He is the author and the finisher of my life. He is first in my life. I fell in love with Jesus. I desired Him, I yearned for Him and the next moment I could spend with Him. I didn't need to be concerned with who I could trust, because I was certain (and am certain) that I could trust God with my heart. His love is never failing.

Jeremiah 31:3-4, says "The Lord appeared to us in the past, saying: I have loved you with an everlasting love; I have drawn you with unfailing kindness. I will build you up again, and you, Virgin Israel, will be rebuilt. Again, you will take up your timbrels and go out to dance with the joyful." Notice the tense of the language here. God reminds us, He *has* loved us, and *will* build you up again. We can trust in the Lord to meet our every need. God tells us we will take up our "timbrels." A timbrel is a tambourine or similar instrument. He promises we will once again sing and dance joyfully; He is our joy.

A little more than two months after that journal entry in October of 2011, wherein I pleaded with God about wanting to be a mother and have a big family, I met my husband, Scott. Scott, was a Master Sargent in the Marine Corps stationed at Patuxent River, living in California, Maryland. I was a Chief of Program Administration and Investment Management for the number one major initiative Program Management Office, for the Department of Veterans Affairs in Washington DC. We were both very busy professionals.

Coincidently, each of us were encouraged by a co-worker to join an online dating site. We both were reluctant but decided to give it a try. Online dating made sense for me because of my current lifestyle. However, if you are considering online dating, let me caution you to do your homework. There are lot of sites to choose from, and there are a lot of dangerous people online. My number one non-negotiable was that I was looking to meet a Christian. I wasn't looking for someone who just professed to believe in Christ, but someone who demonstrated their faith in a daily walk with Christ.

Let's just say God works in mysterious ways (I realize this is a cliché, but it's true). God answered my prayers and responded to that journal entry from October 2011. Scott's four children, plus my two children, are our family with six children (Note – be specific in your prayers; God answers them specifically). I asked for four to six children. This was the desire of my heart. God gave me six children.

So, do you trust in the Lord just because I've told you it's okay? Of course not; trust in the Lord because He said you can. How do you know the Lord says you can trust him? Read His word. Build relationship with Him. It's only through relationship that trust is built.

Lastly, in knowing that you can trust in the Lord, you can trust others. I can be in a relationship and open my heart to others because not matter what happens, my joy comes from the Lord. The Lord is my trust, Jehovah Mibtach. All that I am flows from the Lord. Psalm 23:1-3, says "The Lord is my shepherd, I lack nothing. He makes me lie down in green pastures, he leads me beside quiet waters, he refreshes my soul. He guides me along the right paths for his name sake." We need not want for anything. God provides for us, He guides us, and He is glorified.

CHAPTER 12

JEHOVAH GA'AL, THE LORD
IS MY REDEEMER

I am redeemed! Today, I continue my walk with Christ and every day I draw closer to my Papa. I am victorious! I continue to be amazed by the way God has weaved together every detail of my life and how it has all been for good, and His Glory.

Genesis 50:20 (AMP) says *"As for you, you meant evil against me, but God meant it for good in order to bring about this present outcome, that many people would be kept alive [as they are today]."* I give praise and thanksgiving to God for all that I have experienced in this life thus far; for every struggle, every heartache, every tear, and also every joyous occasion, for laughter and love.

I pray that God will use my story of redemption to bring life, love, laughter, peace and healing to others.

Ephesians 1:7-8, (AMP) says *"In Him we have redemption [that is, our deliverance and salvation] through His blood, [which paid the penalty for our sin and resulted in] the forgiveness and complete pardon of our sin, in accordance with the riches of His grace which He lavished on us. In all wisdom and understanding [with practical insight]."*

The Lord has entrusted much to me. My husband, Scott, and I have been aforded the oportunity and priviledge of providing pastoral care, mentoring and coaching to married couples and families. He has given us a business and continues to grow and prosper us. God has redemed me and trusts me to share my story and His word with you. I'm amazed, humbled and thankful for what the Lord has done in and through me. I stand tall, with my head held high, knowing that I am royalty, the daughter to the King of Kings. I cannot stress enough it is only through Him who strengthens me that I am able to accomplish anything. We must remain in Him daily. When you do, you will soon come to know that spending time with the Lord daily is never a chore, it is a joy. He is my joy.

Not only have I been redeemed, but my family as well. The Lord has poured out His grace, and mercy, blessing and favor. My youngest brother is free from the chains of drug addiction. As I finish this book and write this last chapter, my dad is 27 years sober and my parents recently celebrated 49 years of marriage! When God redeems us, we are made new. The parents I have today are not the same people they were 30 years ago. They have been made new, as have I.

As for Tom, he is deceased now. I don't know what he looks like today, but I do know that Tom is a child of God and there is good in him because of this fact. God is good, and Tom is created in His image. The things Tom did to me were bad, but that doesn't mean Tom is bad. The Lord has given me compassion for Tom. The Lord has revealed to me the darkness that tormented Tom. I pray for his redemption as well.

God has comforted me and been there for me. He has embraced me and wiped away my tears. The Lord has roared like a lion and protected me. The Lord has strengthened me. He is my song and worthy of my praise. The Lord has healed me and poured out His mercy and grace over me. The Lord continues to light my path. He is my salvation. The Lord walks with me and I trust in Him. He has redeemed me. The Lord has given me His name and adopted me as the daughter to the King. He calls me royalty!

EPILOGUE

Mark 1:14-15, says *"After John was put in prison, Jesus went into Galilee, proclaiming the good news of God. "The time has come," he said. "The kingdom of God has come near. Repent and believe the good news!"* God's Kingdom is here.

You are a child of God. You belong to Him. You are loved unconditionally and forgiven for your sins. You are precious in the eyes of our Lord and have been created for a purpose; for His purpose. God tells us in Jeremiah 1:5, *"Before I formed you in the womb I knew you, before you were born I set you apart; I appointed you as a prophet to nations."*

In Matthew 16:15-19, Jesus said to them, "But who do you say that I am?" Simon Peter answered, *"You are the Messiah, the Son of the living God. Jesus replied, "Blessed are you, Simon son of Jonah, for this was not revealed to you by flesh and blood, but by my Father in heaven. And I tell you, that you are Peter, and on this rock, I will build my church, and the gates of Hades will not overcome it. I will give you the keys of the kingdom of heaven, and whatever you bind on earth will be bound in heaven, and whatever you loose on earth will be loosed in heaven."*

Who do you say Jesus is? When you accept Jesus into your heart and receive the Holy Spirit; when you declare that Jesus is the Christ, the Son of the living God, you open a flood gate for receiving His blessing into your life, and you will come to know who you are as well. Knowing your identity in Christ is paramount in finding freedom.

How do we form our identity? Who have you let define your identity? When you are asked to introduce yourself, what do you say? My name is Tina, and I am Scott's wife; I am a mother, a sister, a daughter, a friend ... You get the picture, right? How do you introduce yourself? We describe ourselves, and identify with, the roles we play in life as well as the work we do.

Also, and unfortunately, we often let others tell us who we are. "You're stupid, you're crazy, you're fat, you're ugly, you will never amount to anything"; sound familiar?

Why do we find it so hard to believe what God says about us; who God says we are!? Perhaps you haven't sought His opinion. Do you know who God says you are? Have you accepted Christ as your Lord and Savior? Romans 10:9-10 says, *"If you declare with your mouth, 'Jesus is Lord,' and believe in your heart that God raised him from the dead, you will be saved. For it is with your heart that you believe and are justified, and it is with your mouth that you profess your faith and are saved."* Romans 8:15 says, *"The Spirit you received does not make you slaves, so that you live in fear again, rather, the Spirit you received brought about your adoption to sonship. And by him we cry 'Abba Father.'"*

If you are a believer; if you are a Christian; the Holy Spirit lives in you. If you have not accepted Jesus Christ as your Lord and Savior, I invite you now to do so. Do not wait a moment longer. Put down this book and say aloud the following prayer:

Jesus, I have sinned against you. Please forgive me of my sin. I invite you now into my life and ask that you change my heart. I want you to be Lord over my life, and my Savior. In Jesus name I pray. Amen.

God delights in you and is so pleased you have turned to him. Isaiah 62:5 and 11, says, *"As a young man marries a young woman, so will your Builder marry you; as a bridegroom rejoices over his bride, so will your God rejoice over you." "The Lord has made proclamation to the ends of the earth; 'Say to Daughter Zion, See, your Savior come!"*

The Word says that the Spirit (the Holy Spirit) lives in you and has "brought about your adoption to sonship." This means you are a son or daughter of God's. Romans 8:16 says, *"The Spirit himself testifies with our spirit that we are God's children."* Think about that! You are an heir to the King, the Kingdom of God!

Satan has come to steal, kill and destroy. He is always at work, whispering in our ear to distract us and fix our gaze on what we might see in the flesh. We see the pile of past due bills; the unfavorable medical report; the loss of a loved one; or the signs of drug addiction in a child.

But we know faith comes from hearing, not seeing. Our battle is not with flesh and blood. We are made new in Christ. You are royalty walking about in plain sight. Open your eyes to what God sees; a son or daughter to the King! Listen no more to what society, the media, your "friends," Satan or his minions say about who you are; rather listen to who God says you are. Walk in the light and in favor with him. Receive all God has for you; all he wants to bless you with. The identity crisis is over!

No matter what your story is, what you have done, what might have been done to you …. You are loved, forgiven, belong and have purpose. My hope, and my prayer, is that you hear me; really hear me, and come to know and love God. God has many names that reveal His identity in every situation and every promise He has made. We find comfort, strength, healing, shelter, and much more in each of His names. I pray you will come to understand your identity is found in His name; and that every answer to every question you have, healing for your wounds and comfort for your hurt is found only in Him and His precious and powerful name.

SCRIPTURE REFERENCES

Chapter 1 Jehovah (yeh-ho-vaw') Nacham (naw-kham'), The Lord is my Comforter

Isaiah 66:12-13 NIV

Isaiah 51:11-12 NIV

Chapter 2 Jehovah (yeh-ho-vaw') Shammah (sham-maw'), The Lord is There

Colossians 1:27 NIV

1 Corinthians 3:11-16 NIV

Ezekiel 48:35 NIV

Chapter 3 Jehovah (yeh-ho-vaw') Abba (aba), The Lord our

Father

Isaiah 64:8 NIV

Matthew 14:36 NIV

Romans 8:15 NIV

Psalm 147:3 & 11 NIV

2 Corinthians 3:17 NIV

Romans 12:2 NIV

Chapter 4 Jehovah (yeh-ho-vaw') Sha'ag Tsiyown (shaw-ag' tsee-yone'), The Lord Shall Roar Out of Zion

Joel 3:16 &18 NIV

John 2:13-16 NIV

Ephesians 4:26-27 NLT

Chapter 5 Jehovah (yeh-ho-vaw') Owz Zimrath (oze zim-rawth'), The Lord is My Strength and My Song

Isaiah 61:1-3 ESV

2 Kings 3:14-15 AMP

Chapter 6 Jahovah (yeh-ho-vaw') Rapha (raw-faw'), The Lord Your Healer

1 Peter 2:9 NIV

Exodus 16:26 NIV

Luke 15:11-24 ESV

Chapter 7 Jahovah (yeh-ho-vaw') Checed (kheh'-sed), The Lord is Merciful and Gracious

Jeremiah 29:11 NIV

Nehemiah 9:17 ESV

Ephesians 4:31-32 NIV

Ephesians 6:10-12 AMP

Ephesians 6:13-16 AMP

Ephesians 6:18 AMP

Ephesians 1:7 AMP

Philippians 3:13-14 NIV

2 Corinthians 5:17 ESV

Chapter 8 Jehovah (yeh-ho-vaw') Halal (haw-lal'), The Lord is Worthy to be Praised

Matthew 28:19-20 AMP

Matthew 19:26 NIV

Chapter 9 Jehovah (yeh-ho-vaw') Owr (ore) Yesha (yay'-shah), The Lord is my Light and my Salvation

Psalm 27:1-9 AMP

John 19:30 NIV

Chapter 10   Jehovah (yeh-ho-vaw') Immanuel (im-maw-noo-ale'), The Lord God is With Us

Isaiah 7:14 AMP

Chapter 11 Jehovah (yeh-ho-vaw') Mibtach (mib-tawkh') The Lord is my Trust

Psalm 71:5-6 NIV

Jeremiah 34:3-4 NIV

Psalm 23:1-3 NIV

Chapter 12 Jehovah (yeh-ho-vaw') Ga'al (gaw-al'), The Lord is my Redeemer

Genesis 50:20 AMP

Ephesians 1:7-8 AMP

Epilogue

Mark 1:14-15 NIV

Jeremiah 1:5 NIV

Matthew 16:15-19 NIV

Romans 10:9-10 NIV

Romans 8:15 NIV

Isaiah 62:5 & 11 NIV

Romans 8:16 NIV

ABOUT THE AUTHOR

Tina Adams

Tina Adams is a Christian Author from Louisiana. She currently resides in Mobile, AL with her husband Scott Adams. Tina is passionate about sharing the gospel and helping people understand their identity as a child of God. Her greatest desire and prayer in writing this book and sharing her story, is that it will bless any woman who has ever struggled with their self-worth and identity, and most importantly, bring honor and glory to God.

Follow Tina on Facebook:
@ChristianAuthorTinaAdams